GARDEN CITY STATE

SLOW INFRASTRUCTURE FOR NEW JERSEY

MARIO GANDELSONAS
PHILIP TIDWELL

A PUBLICATION OF THE PRINCETON UNIVERSITY
CENTER FOR ARCHITECTURE, URBANISM AND INFRASTRUCTURE

Published by the
CENTER FOR
ARCHITECTURE,
URBANISM
+ INFRASTRUCTURE
SCHOOL OF ARCHITECTURE
PRINCETON UNIVERSITY
S-110 ARCHITECTURE BUILDING
PRINCETON, NJ 08544-5264
W CAUI.PRINCETON.EDU
E URBANISM@PRINCETON.EDU

Distributed by
Island Press
2000 M Street, NW
Suite 650
Washington, DC 20036
www.islandpress.org

Series Editor: Mario Gandelsonas
Book Editors: Mario Gandelsonas, Philip Tidwell
Design: Philip Tidwell
Managing Editor: Nancy Later
Copy Editor: Linda Lee
Printer: Asia Pacific Offset

Printed and bound in China.

ISBN: 978-0-9886663-1-3

CONTENTS

INTRODUCTION 4
Mario Gandelsonas, Philip Tidwell

SLOW INFRASTRUCTURE 8
Mario Gandelsonas

AMERICA 2050: 28
INFRASTRUCTURE AND URBANISM AT THE SCALE OF THE MEGAREGION
Petra Todorovich Messick

GARDEN [CITY] STATE 40
Philip Tidwell

NEW JERSEY TOWNS 44
Tom Wright

A SPECULATIVE ATLAS 52
Matthew Clarke, Willem Boning, Phoebe Springstubb, Sam Stewart-Halevy, Philip Tidwell, Stephanie Lee, Cong Wang, Lydia Xynogala

INTRODUCTION

MARIO GANDELSONAS
PHILIP TIDWELL

In 2010, 81 percent of Americans lived in cities. By 2016 that number is expected to rise to as high as 90 percent. In this context New Jersey might be seen as a logical conclusion—rather than an anomalous exception—to the long trajectory of American urbanism. With fragmentary planning and an extensive network of automobile-based transportation, the state has, since the 2008 mortgage crisis and subsequent economic slowdown, continued its relentless growth with only slight impedance. Already the most densely settled state in the nation, New Jersey will be the first to exhaust its territorial resources and cover 100 percent of available land with sprawling, low-density urbanization. Precisely what this means is open for debate, but it is clear that the aging and already strained infrastructure of the state will be subjected to even greater social, economic, and environmental pressures. As the force of these pressures increases, it is difficult to believe that things will continue to function according to standard operating procedures.

The dramatic effects of Hurricane Sandy in 2012 pose only the most visible of the many challenges facing New Jersey today. From the Atlantic shore to the Delaware River, a multitude of systems, structures, and urban areas across the state must be reinforced and rebuilt. During the next forty years, billions of dollars will be invested to treat water, deliver energy, and insure personal mobility, but if these investments only result in a return to the status quo, the long-term future of the region will remain uncertain. The continued viability of the Garden State depends not only on repairing and renewing its infrastructure but also reconsidering the role of infrastructure itself from the ground up.

Garden [City] State takes a wide perspective on these challenges in order to propose new infrastructures that will adapt to the state's particular landscape and exploit its urban condition. The proposal takes as its starting point the framework developed by the America 2050 initiative, a national effort spearheaded by the Regional Plan Association to direct American urban development in the coming decades. Key to this effort is the identification of eleven emerging *megaregions*, within which most population growth is projected to occur. These large, networked metropolitan areas form the new units of urban governance, infrastructure, and land-use planning. They serve not only as geographic demarcations but also conceptual tools, which can be used to address urban growth and sprawl at a new scale. By shaping new investments in infrastructure such as the federal High-Speed Intercity Passenger Rail Program along megaregional lines, America 2050 will help realize the economic promise of the nation.

But for these megaregions to reach their full potential, it will be necessary to restructure and expand existing systems, as well as create new ones. Our project explores ways of upending the traditional logic of territorial expansion developed during the nineteenth and twentieth centuries and transitioning from the fast, hard infrastructure of the freeway, the electric grid, and the impervious watershed—which all served as a precondition for sprawl—toward an emerging infrastructure of the twenty-first century. This new infrastructure supports slow mobility systems, soft digital technologies, and the couplings that connect the two. So while the future infrastructure of the megaregion may include high-speed rail, that system will be complemented by a slower mobility network, which combines new developments in technology and computation with distributed energy systems and soft watersheds.

As the 2010 U.S. Census confirmed, the growth rate of New Jersey has now eclipsed that of its metropolitan neighbors: throughout the next decade, the state will incur a startling proportion of the megaregion's growth (see page 52). Whereas today 8.8 million people live in the state, by 2050, 10 million people may call it home.[2] Where these additional 1.2 million residents will choose to live depends largely upon decisions made today. If appropriate measures are not taken, new residents will continue to settle outside of existing urban centers, where new transportation, water, and energy infrastructures will consume land and environmental resources unnecessarily in order to support them. A major goal of the *Garden [City] State* proposal is to anticipate and direct growth in a way that conserves the state's environmental resources. More than just bucolic vistas, the forest, wetland, and coastal areas of New Jersey that are currently at risk for overdevelopment must be revalued as essential tools for dealing with the increased frequency and intensity of flooding and severe weather.

With a particular focus on the southern half of the state, the proposal identifies twelve towns outside the perimeter of the protected Pinelands region toward which growth should be directed. These towns are to be woven together by a greenway loop of slow infrastructure that connects directly to a triangulated system of high-speed transport. The term *greenway* is meant to stand not only for vegetation—as this is an essential component—but also for a broad plurality of recreational activities that incorporate the body in motion. The intention is to create a space of total continuity and connectivity for pedestrians, bicycles, and low-speed transportation that parallels the existing world of connectivity created for the car (highways, parkways, streets, etc.). The greenway loop provides a continuous ground that reconnects the fragmented world of the pedestrian to the main streets of adjacent towns, existing green areas, and even formerly car-dependent shopping malls and residential clusters. The greenway is imagined as an "other" place, outside the air-conditioned, hermetically-sealed, policed interiors of office complexes and retail stores, where we can disentangle ourselves from the network of surrogate public space and recapture a genuine, daily experience of the ground under our feet.

Could this case study be projected to the wider context of the megaregion and be adapted to other settings, modalities, and conditions that have the potential to be developed as a slow infrastructure? The hard infrastructures of the twentieth century need to be transformed and coupled with the new slow and soft infrastructures of the twenty-first century to produce multifunctional territories for habitation and agriculture, transportation and energy, industry and pleasure. In contrast to strict technocratic management, twenty-first-century urbanization requires negotiation between the needs of transportation and mobile accessibility on the one hand and the sometimes-competing requirements of energy and water systems on the other; it requires balancing the demands of a productive agricultural and industrial landscape with the needs of humans, animals, and plants for landscapes of pleasure and identity.

Slow infrastructure proposes that we expand what can be thought of as infrastructure and seek to become more precise in our delineation of the virtues of specific infrastructural components and operations. Infrastructural design must be positioned to encompass a variety of roles, from *programming* social interactions, ecological processes, and resource mobilizations to *translating* operations present across a range of scales, audiences, and material languages. This proposal should be considered a first step that could inform the future of the infrastructural project as a determinant force in the creation of new sites for urbanism and architectural intervention.

NOTES
1 Based on research by the U.S. Bureau of Labor Statistics compiled in the New Jersey Division of Labor Market and Demographic Research, *New Jersey Employment and Population in the 21st Century* (Trenton: 2008), 8-9.
2 "Projections of the Population by Selected Age Groups and Sex for the United States: 2015 to 2060" last modified May 7, 2013, http://www.census.gov/population/projections/files/summary/NP2012-T2.csv

SLOW
INFRASTRUCTURE

MARIO GANDELSONAS

Originally published by Princeton Architectural Press in
Fast Forward Urbanism, Dana Cuff, editor, New York, 2011

The infrastructure built in the United States in the first half of the twentieth century is crumbling. We are at a point in history where the problems caused by deferred maintenance have produced a number of major disasters. The August, 2007, rush-hour collapse of a six-hundred-foot bridge along highway I-35W in Minneapolis that killed thirty people is only one in a long list. In May of 2003, the Silver Lake Dam in Michigan failed, causing one hundred million dollars in damages. Two years later, the inadequacies of the levees in New Orleans became horrifyingly clear in the aftermath of Hurricane Katrina in August of 2005. Only a month before the Minneapolis bridge collapse, a hundred-year-old steam pipe had erupted in Midtown Manhattan, causing millions of dollars in lost business. These events have led to questioning of the inaction leading to this situation, and increased calls for the repair and expansion of existing infrastructure.[1]

However, the problem goes beyond maintenance. The tendency to associate the term "infrastructure" with public works from the twentieth-century prevents us from addressing the urgent need to rethink the very idea of infrastructure itself. Radical changes in telecommunications and "telemediatization," following the development of new technologies of media, communication, and information processing, have begun to challenge our understanding of our infrastructures—in particular those related to transportation—and the cultures associated with them.[2]

America's crumbling infrastructure is the manifestation of the early-twentieth-century European architectural avant-garde's notion of urbanism. Modern urbanists, most notably Le Corbusier, fantasized about replacing the

Throughout New Jersey, most residential developments—in spite of
their geographic proximity—are separated by a fragmentary network of
undeveloped land.

dark, tortuous streets of the old cities with a new city that would welcome the sudden appearance of the machine, and, more specifically, the car. The modernist city was organized on the basis of the oppositional separation of drivers and pedestrians to facilitate the fluid movement of the automobile. The old city streets were seen as obstacles to movement that should be surgically removed.

The very same European cities that were seen as impediments to progress by the modernists also shaped our notion of an urban culture, which is embodied in an infrastructure of urban rooms, streets, and alleys.[3] The role of this urban infrastructure had always been to allow for the movement of people, goods, and information, and therefore to provide accessibility and contact. It took centuries to restructure the existing labyrinth of urban streets and alleys into a network of wide streets and boulevards to allow for more fluid movement. This began with Pope Sixtus V's restructuring of Rome at the end of the sixteenth century, with new avenues linking churches to allow for the flow of religious processions, and culminated in the late nineteenth century, with major European capitals being reworked into networks of avenues that slashed through the old medieval fabric, providing more direct access to cultural and political institutions. Train terminals occupied an important space in this network, marking the symbolic presence of the mechanical revolution in the form of the railroad.

Modernist urbanism, based in the hard technologies of the late-nineteenth-/early-twentieth-century mechanical revolution, promoted new urban concepts such as the grid, the highway, and the superblock. These new concepts would completely replace the fabric of the old European city and allow the uninterrupted movement and high speed of the car to replace the slow speed of the pedestrian. Modernist urbanism was the result of the mutual reshaping of the urban culture of mechanical modernism and the physical city. On both sides of the Atlantic, changes in infrastructure, most notably the highway system and suburbanization, affected both the physical city and urban culture. In particular, the U.S. freeway system is one of the most important infrastructural works of the twentieth century and constitutes the best example of the change in urban form as the result of changes in infrastructure. Overdetermined by the Cold War and the possibility of

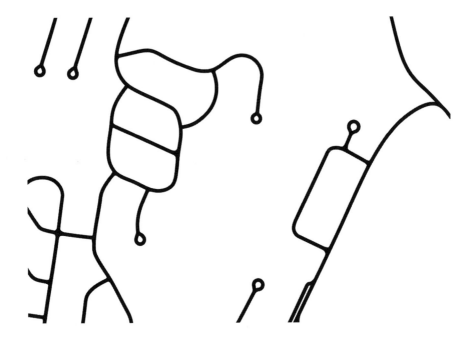

Today, the only means of movement between most neighborhoods is along labyrinthine roads via the inefficient maneuvering of the personal car. In order to reconfigure this organization, we look at the backside or backyard of these housing areas.

nuclear warfare, the National System of Interstate and Defense Highways was built to implement the strategy of dispersal under the directives of the National Industrial Dispersion Program, which planned for survival after an atomic attack. Laid out by highway designers in consultation with federal civil defense agencies, the highway system was inspired by the German Autobahn, built in the thirties. The American highway system is still completely embedded in our urban life and consciousness as the infrastructural backbone of mid-century suburbanization.

However, for the last fifteen years we have entered a different situation characterized by a new condition of accessibility. Twentieth-century infrastructure allowed physical mobility based on the hard technologies of the mechanical revolution that dominated the previous century. In contrast, today's softer technologies—of electronic information processing and of media and communication systems—are generating new possibilities of interaction and contact for the production, reception, and distribution of information. The processing of information had always been a unique role offered by cities, but the accelerated growth of telemediated activities has generated a radical change in the way we understand and practice accessibility. New values, experiences, and emerging fantasies are producing what has been called a new culture of immediacy. "Watching television, typing, scrolling, clicking, and browsing at the computer screen, talking, texting, or sending and receiving pictures on a mobile phone; tapping in PIN codes and conducting transactions on the keypad [of an ATM] although so much a routine and taken for granted should be seen as cultural practices."

With the introduction of the latest information and communication devices, new couplings are produced between the new media, old media, hard infrastructure, the physical city, and the body. In fact, the vast spaces of train terminals represent the physical relationship between the railroad—the nineteenth-century hard infrastructure of transportation—and the city. While the coupling between the train and the city accelerates the latter's growth and density without modifying its structure in a substantial way, the articulation of the city and the car, which takes place through the coupling of the house and the car, radically breaks away from the known city, creating a completely new urbanity.

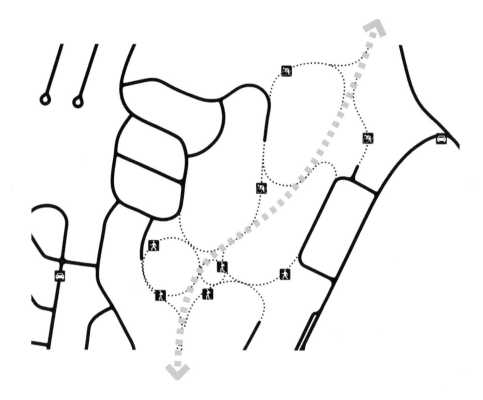

In the leftover space between these two neighborhoods, there is an opportunity to introduce low-impact public transit. A series of slow recreational loops could provide access to a central smart transit loop, with buses or light-rail transit where land is available.

This new urbanity, promoted by the dominance of the cars that rapidly replaced public transportation, also involves a third territory: the old media. The articulation between physical spaces and media started in the early twentieth century with the joining of the house, the telephone, and the radio—a coupling that had been dominant prior to World War II. [7] The growing dominance of the automobile in the mid-twentieth century established a new paradigm: the car as a mobile private space entwined with the fixed spaces of the city, and in particular with the house as well as the contemporary media. The coupling of the house and the radio was transformed by the introduction of the car and the television: the TV occupied the place of the radio within the house and displaced the radio to the car. A profound symbolic restructuring took place, where the logic of the supplement eventually supplanted what it was supposed to augment. [8] In the suburban context, the TV began to take the place of the central city and the car started to supplant the house.

Neither the mid-twentieth-century media nor the couplings mentioned above presupposed the obsolescence of the old media; the newer media altered the relationships established by the old media and at the same time, produced new ones. The physical/spatial city was also altered: old downtowns were radically transformed by the flight to the rapidly expanding suburbs, which soon surpassed the downtowns in size. Over the last fifteen years, new media technologies, like the personal computer, and associated practices have undermined the mid-twentieth-century paradigm and are now starting to produce the first new couplings of an emerging, early-twenty-first-century paradigm. The rituals of the television culture and collective reception of the 1950s (where the TV set was the focus of the family) are being replaced by rituals of a new culture of immediacy that is composed of new structures of social networking and forms of producing, consuming, exchanging, and archiving information. [9]

How are the media technologies integrating with patterns of physical mobility and space in the fluid, light modernity in which we live? Telemediatization is not promoting a sedentary life, as urban theorist Melvin Webber predicted in the 1960s and as urbanist Paul Virilio has argued more recently. [10] Rather, telemediatization has dynamically integrated an

These slower recreational loops provide convenient alternatives to the individually navigated car. The central public transit bridges cul-de-sac outposts and provides transit continuity.

increasingly mobile population into a "fluid modernity." It is fluid because contemporary culture is unfolding in the movement of the restless streets of the busy metropolis rather than in the isolated, controlled, and serviced environment of a wired dwelling. Beginning in the early twentieth century, the house functioned as a center for information management, first through radio and telephone and then through television. The increased mobility provided by the coupling of the latest technologies and the body has caused a shift in the role of the house, which has become the fixed personal center of telemediated activities where the "heavier" infrastructure is located, such as servers, large-screen televisions, and high-speed, wired connections to the internet.[11] How does the new media technology change the imagined relationship to the places we inhabit? The constant switching—from radio to TV to music player, to email and to internet browsing, to computer and to phone—is an activity not just associated with the stable, fixed place of the office or home but now commonly projected onto the public or semipublic spaces of the city.

While the introduction of the car produced radical changes in urban structure, the rise of new technologies is causing a similar shift in the role of the car as the dominant means of transportation in the United States. In fact, the car is incompatible with the perceptual demands of telemediatization. On the other hand, public transportation, such as the train and the airplane, are rapidly adapting to these new demands. The incompatibility of driving and telemediatization presupposes the need for forms of transportation that allow the mobile twenty-first-century individual to maintain contact.[12] The transportation needs of the mobile, telemediated individual will certainly promote in the middle and long term a fundamental restructuring of cities themselves.[13]

In the twenty-first century, it is the notion of mobility itself that is changing. For example, Virilio argues that there has been a shift in emphasis from the physical mobility of people and objects through physical space to the virtual mobility of signal input and output, and from departure to arrival within electronic space. As opposed to the coupling between infrastructure and the city represented by the monumental train terminals of the mechanical revolution, a new relationship exists between the new soft

Car Share

Green Line

At the scale of the individual, transportation options for a trip to the local supermarket or the nearest hardware store are increased dramatically.

technologies and the body. The new terminals cease to be fixed points in physical space organizing our patterns of mobility. We carry them with, and perhaps soon within, ourselves.[14] Each of us is a potential terminal. This transformation is made possible as the easy communication of the mobile phone morphs into a mini handheld computer, social networking device, and tiny, individual movie screen. The new technology, effortless and ever-present, appears to close the gap preserved by the mechanical revolution between here and elsewhere, now and later, desire and fulfillment.[15]

The coupling between new technology and the body also has major implications at the social level, and in particular at the economic level, where cities behave as economic engines. For example, the new global economy contains electronically based communities of individuals and organizations that interact in the nonphysical, nonspatial, electronic realm. The internet enables these economic actors to relate to each other in real time, seemingly disregarding the fixed spaces of the physical cities around them.

Despite its pervasiveness, this new economic geography is only one fragmented moment in a vast chain of events that remain embedded in nonelectronic spaces that are never fully dematerialized.[16] Digitization has not eliminated the need for spaces and infrastructure, but has fostered a dispersal of activities that can be developed independent of any fixed physical location. In most instances this dynamic has contributed to the most negative aspects of exurban growth: the internet exchanges in buildings for clusters of servers and the groups of scaleless distribution centers, built in places such as Woodbridge and other New Jersey towns, but also all over exurban America. The counterpart of the dispersal promoted by the digital is a new logic for the aggregation of activities. An example of this are the forms of articulation of people and territory revealed by the patterns of spatial centralization in the dense new suburban subcenters, correlated to the continuing growth of the exurban city.[17]

Perhaps the most profound implication of this paradigmatic change takes place in the restructuring of the experience of urban contact. The accidental physical encounter—the quintessential attribute of the urban realm—had been greatly reduced in twentieth-century American cities because of the dominance of the car as a mode of transportation and the

By glancing at a tablet or smartphone, residents can locate the next bus
that will come through their backyard greenway and compare this with
the closest distance to their local car and bike share.

type of urbanization it promoted. Instead, we saw an increase in various forms of attenuated contact, such as visual interaction between drivers and the violent contact of the car accident, which has been described as an accidental, physical encounter fostered by the suburban and the contemporary exurban city.[18] In fact, since the mid-twentieth century the possibilities for this kind of interaction, opened by twentieth-century infrastructure, have increased exponentially, while the possibilities for face-to-face contact have been greatly reduced, first with the development of the suburban city and then in the last twenty-five years by the new diffuse, scattered, and ever-expanding exurban city.

Another type of attenuated contact that has increased exponentially is the digital encounter promoted by the internet. Some of the constraints of human embodiment have been overcome by the coupling of the new teletechnologies and the body/subject: first, because of the portability of new media and the perception that the world moves along with the individual at its center, and second, because of the phenomenon of telepresence and the resulting condition of immediacy that has created an apparent closure of the gap between people. However, the immediacy of contact limited to the modality of electronic communication is not supplanting face-to-face contacts, but seems to complement them.[19] Although the recent development of internet-based social networking (on sites like Facebook and MySpace) would first seem to work against the survival, persistence, and growth of face-to-face interactions, the opposite seems to be true, as seen, for example, in the increased popularity of libraries in the last few years, a situation that has accelerated with the current financial crisis.[20]

Contact is precisely what provides social enjoyment and the high returns that make urban life truly rich. For this reason, the desire for a coupling between new technology and spaces that offer opportunities for and facilitate contact—both the accidental physical encounter and the digital encounter allowed by teletechnologies—will continue to grow as well. The accelerating increase in the use of libraries, the exponential growth of cafes in the last few years (both independent and owned by corporations), and the proliferation of indoor and outdoor places for physical activity illustrate different forms of this new desire for contact. And mobility is increasing as

By the same means of their smartphone or locator, they can signal a greenway bus, and as several neighbors do the same, their collective desire motions the bus to stop in their vicinity.

well: the new connectedness is increasing both internet traffic and real traffic, in particular because the new social networks include people who do not live nearby and therefore travel to connect. The constraints of the physical world, of the embodied human condition, and ultimately of the exurban city are contributing to the continuous growth of the vast contemporary economy of transportation in Americ,a with a growing emphasis on trains and light-rail.[21]

What will the infrastructure that serves the new culture of immediacy be? What would be the twenty-first-century equivalent of the mid-twentieth century Interstate and Defense Highway system? Current trends point to the creation of a new slow infrastructure: public transportation that can perform as a "mobile base" for the millions of body-terminals that are constantly plugged into the new soft electronic infrastructure. The new slow, or soft, infrastructure that traverses every one of the eleven megaregions proposed by the Regional Plan Association will be connected to a restructured, augmented, and expanded twenty-first-century fast, and hard, infrastructure.[22] While the restructured, hard infrastructure will consolidate the megaregions and link them together at a national level using high-speed trains, buses, and airlines, a new slow infrastructure will organize the multiple scales within the different megaregions (from microscale to macroscale, i.e., from the neighborhood to the town, city, metropolis, and megaregion). This slow infrastructure will also restructure the green and open spaces, provide alternative energy, manage the waters, and allow for a multiplicity of movement systems that will support the millions of body-terminals. Architects and urban designers should be assigned the urgent task of finding public moments and spaces where interaction and contact with others are possible and developing the strategies and tactics needed to inhabit these emerging public spaces.

The new slow infrastructure proposes a displacement from the spatial to the temporal, from strict functionality to a multiplicity of overlapping activities and spaces of enjoyment. This displacement opens up new possibilities with respect to the object and the subject of infrastructure. This is particularly true for the new twenty-first-century body: a body that has been restructured in the last twenty years with prosthetic extensions and

This interface of mobility infrastructure and digital technology has the potential to reorder and restructure time. Rather than being schedule dependent, residents can select the mode of mobility that is readily available and suits their lifestyle.

connecting fields that have constantly and continuously reinvented it.[23] Rethinking the object of infrastructure will displace the exclusive focus on the kind of accessibility that is provided by physical mobility, and replace that focus with an awareness of the new telemediated accessibility that constitutes the culture of immediacy. Rethinking infrastructure will also promote the study of possibilities for articulating new twenty-first-century infrastructure inside, on top of, beneath, and beside hard twentieth-century infrastructure. It will also create new sites for architectural intervention, for the design and implementation of new types of sustainable, slow infrastructure from the local level to the national level of the megaregions.

EPILOGUE: INFRASTRUCTURE OF URBAN ENJOYMENT

The construction of the railroad during the nineteenth century produced one of the most important changes in the spatial and social organization of the United States: the generation of a new urbanity. Every stop of the New Jersey Transit rail lines, for instance, encouraged urban growth. However, the demise of a number of routes and services during the mid-twentieth century produced a no man's land that pierced through towns and cities, fragmenting them and separating neighborhoods. Service cuts also produced a reserve of undeveloped land—an opportunity uncovered with the South Amboy Greenway project, developed by Agrest and Gandelsonas Architects in 2005.

The South Amboy Greenway recuperates 340 acres of undeveloped land adjacent to the railroad in the city of South Amboy, a stop on the New Jersey Transit rail. The project proposes a transformation of the old, fast infrastructure of the railroad into a new type of slow infrastructure: a green zone for walking, jogging, biking, rollerblading, skateboarding, and horseback riding articulated by public spaces and sports and cultural facilities, all powered by solar panels and clusters of wind turbines.

At the physical level, the greenway sutures the cut inflicted by the railroad, stitching together the neighborhoods that have been split from the downtown area. At the social level, the transformation of the urban object— the undeveloped land adjacent to the railroad—produces a transformation of the subject—the twenty-first-century urban actor and viewer—by providing new "activity nodes," articulating continuously flowing green vectors, and linking new viewing positions that completely change the perception of the city.

NOTES

1 Bob Herbert, "Our Crumbling Foundation," *New York Times*, 5 Apr. 2007.

2 Telemediatization is defined as modes of electronic communication and media that together have fundamentally transformed global connectivity, time-space relations, and cultural experience. Telemediated practices include internet surfing, instant messaging, tweeting, Google-based research, television, texting, mobile phone photo-sharing, web-based social networking, and so on. See John Tomlinson, "Globalization and Cultural Analysis," in *Globalization Theory: Approaches and Controversy*, ed. David Held and Anthony McGrew (New York: Polity, 2007), 148–68.

3 This text does not consider the less visible infrastructure (e.g., water, sewer, utilities, and so on) in order to focus on mobility in its relationship to accessibility and urbanity.

4 Peter Galison, "War Against the Center," *Grey Room* 4 (Summer 2001): 25.

5 John Tomlinson, *The Culture of Speed: The Coming of Immediacy* (Los Angeles: Sage Publications, 2007); see also Paul Virilio, *Open Sky*, trans. Julie Rose (New York: Verso, 1997). There have been two successive technological revolutions in mobility: the late-nineteenth- and early-twentieth-century transportation revolution and the late-twentieth- and early-twenty-first-century communications and media technologies revolution.

6 Tomlinson, *The Culture of Speed*, 94.

7 Mario Gandelsonas, *X-Urbanism* (New York: Princeton Architectural Press, 1999).

8 Jacques Derrida, *De la Grammatologie* (Paris, Éditions de Minuit, 1967); see also Jacques Derrida, *Of Grammatology*, trans. Gayatri Chakravorty Spivak (Baltimore, MD: Johns Hopkins University Press, 1976).

9 Particularly for teenagers, telemediated activities and the related management of information are occupying an increasing amount of time, while the time devoted to the car and television are rapidly decreasing. The number of teenagers using the internet grew 24 percent between 2001 and 2005 and is only continuing to climb, while the national rate of licensed sixteen-year-olds dropped to 29.8 percent in 2006 from 43.8 percent in 1998 according to the Federal Highway Administration. Mary M. Chapman and Micheline Maynard, "Fewer Youths Jump Behind the Wheel at 16," *New York Times*, 25 Feb. 2008.

10 Melvin Webber, "Urban Place and Nonplace Urban Realm," in *Explorations into Urban Structure* (Philadelphia: University of Pennsylvania Press, 1964).

11 See Diana Agrest, "The Misfortunes of Theory," in *Architecture from Without: Theoretical Framings for a Critical Practice* (Cambridge, MA: MIT Press, 1991).

12 The dangers of driving while using cell phones for calls or texting is increasingly leading states to prohibit cell phone use by drivers. Similarly, some teenagers prefer to be driven by parents so they can keep texting their friends, or even text friends in the car with them to avoid being overheard. See Laura M. Holson, "Text Generation

Gap: UR 2 Old (JK)," *New York Times*, 9 Mar. 2008.

13 "As metropolitan regions continued to expand throughout the second half of the 20th century their boundaries began to blur, creating a new scale of geography now known as the megaregion." America 2050, "Megaregions," http://www.america2050.org/megaregions.html, accessed 30 Aug. 2009.

14 I am paraphrasing Virilio, Open Sky, 9–25.

15 Ibid.

16 Saskia Sassen, *The Global City: New York, London, Tokyo* (Princeton, NJ: Princeton University Press, 1991).

17 The 2004 U.S. Census describes the new suburban "centers" developed by Latino communities in Atlanta, Georgia.

18 Mario Gandelsonas, introduction to *In Search of the Public*, a publication from the Center for Architecture, Urbanism, and Infrastructure at Princeton University; see also Jon Garvie, "Who lives by the road, dies by the road," in *Times Online*, 3 Dec. 2008, http://entertainment.timesonline.co.uk/tol/arts_and_entertainment/the_tls/article5278712.ece.

19 Jeffrey Boase, John Horrigan, Barry Wellman, and Lee Rainie, "The Strength of Internet Ties," *Pew Internet & American Life Project*, 25 Jan. 2006, http://www.pewinternet.org/Reports/2006/The-Strength-of-Internet-Ties.aspx?r=1.

20 Contrary to fears that email would reduce other forms of contact, there is "media multiplexity": the more contact by email, the more in-person and phone contact. As a result, Americans are probably more in contact with members of their communities and social networks than before the advent of the internet. Ibid.

21 "With $8 billion in federal stimulus money allocated for passenger rail projects, the States for Passenger Rail Coalition foresees the beginning of a new era of expanded intercity passenger rail service throughout America. The projects will expand and enhance passenger rail service in multiple ways, while creating thousands of new, good-paying jobs across the nation. In addition, President Obama has indicated that another $5 billion can be expected over the next five years, from the administration's proposed transportation budget." Trains for America, "States Expect Rail Growth," 18 Mar. 2009. http://trains4america.wordpress.com/?s=states+expect+train+growth&searchbutton=go! These projects could be considered the first step in the consolidations of the megaregions (see note 13).

22 "Most of the nation's rapid population growth, and an even larger share of its economic expansion, is expected to occur in 10 or more emerging megaregions: large networks of metropolitan regions, each megaregion covering thousands of square miles and located in every part of the country….The recognition of the megaregion as an emerging geographical unit also presents an opportunity to reshape large federal systems of infrastructure and funding….Just as the Interstate Highway System enabled the growth of metropolitan regions during the second half of the 20th century, emerging megaregions will require new transportation modes that work for places 200–500 miles across." America 2050, "Megaregions."

23 Donna Jeanne Haraway, "A Cyborg Manifesto: Science, Technology, and Socialist-Feminism in the Late Twentieth Century," in *Simians, Cyborgs, and Women: The Reinvention of Nature* (New York: Routledge, 1991), 149–81.

AMERICA 2050: INFRASTRUCTURE AND URBANISM AT THE SCALE OF THE MEGAREGION

PETRA TODOROVICH MESSICK

Created by the Regional Plan Association in 2005, America 2050 is a national initiative that addresses the infrastructure, economic development, and environmental challenges faced by the United States as it prepares for a population increase of approximately 130 million during the next forty years. Lead by the National Committee for America 2050, a coalition of regional planners, scholars, and policy makers, the initiative has developed a wide body of research on subjects ranging from urban sprawl and climate change to foreign trade and economic growth. Among the most important efforts of America 2050 is the identification and concentration of effort on eleven emerging megaregions in the nation. These megaregions constitute large networks of urbanization, where most of the population growth in the next four decades is expected to take place.

In one sense, these megaregions are the American response to a global condition. In Europe and Southeast Asia, governments are investing tens of billions of dollars in systems designed to move people and goods across networks of cities in "global integration zones." In the United States, megaregions are expected to compete with their international counterparts and to serve as the new, competitive units in the global economy.

But in another important way, the idea of the megaregion as an urban entity marks an important conceptual shift in our way of thinking about American cities. Today our urban agglomerations are related only loosely to the political borders that define their administration. The megaregion shifts our conception of the city from a singular entity to a multitude of metropolitan areas connected by overlapping commuting patterns, business travel, environmental landscapes and watersheds, economies, and social networks. By necessity it spans local and state boundaries. As the notion of the American city becomes less monolithic and increasingly dispersed, so too do its systems of governance and planning. Strategies for economic regeneration, transportation, and sustainable growth must be deployed at a larger scale to transition from an industrial to an information-based economy.

HIGH-SPEED RAIL

A central component of the American 2050 plan and the idea behind the megaregion is the ability to move both people and goods freely between urban hubs. This depends on the development of fast and reliable rail transportation, which is achievable by improving existing corridors as well as developing new high-speed links between urban centers. The rationale is that as each megaregion reduces its dependency on less efficient systems (auto and air travel), its capacity for growth will increase.

But in an era of austerity and economic uncertainty, the long lead time and inherent risk involved in high-speed rail development must be negotiated carefully. In order to minimize investment risk, it is essential to select corridors where the conditions supporting strong passenger demand for high-speed services already exist. To identify these corridors, America 2050 developed a ranking system to assess the extent of demand for high-speed rail between city pairs. By examining approximately six hundred urban centers with a minimum population of fifty thousand, city pairs were created by connecting each city to every other city located within one hundred and five hundred miles. This yielded approximately 27,000 city pairs across the nation which were assessed in reference to six categories: transit connections, population, location, proximity, economic vitality, and congestion. These variables were weighted and then summed into an index that scored all city pairs.

THE FUTURE OF AMERICA 2050

Since the launch of the program, America 2050 has published research and made policy recommendations on key issues impacting the future growth and competitive edge of the United States. Between 2008 and 2009, it

hosted major conferences in eight different megaregions to identify stra-
tegic infrastructure priorities for a national infrastructure plan. Since 2009
the program has shaped the national debate on high-speed rail and recom-
mended ways in which national investments should be focused within corridors that show the greatest demand for ridership. In the coming years,
America 2050 will continue to provide leadership on regional planning and
national infrastructure priorities, while also addressing water and energy
planning and land-use considerations.

AMERICA 2050:
THE EMERGING MEGAREGIONS

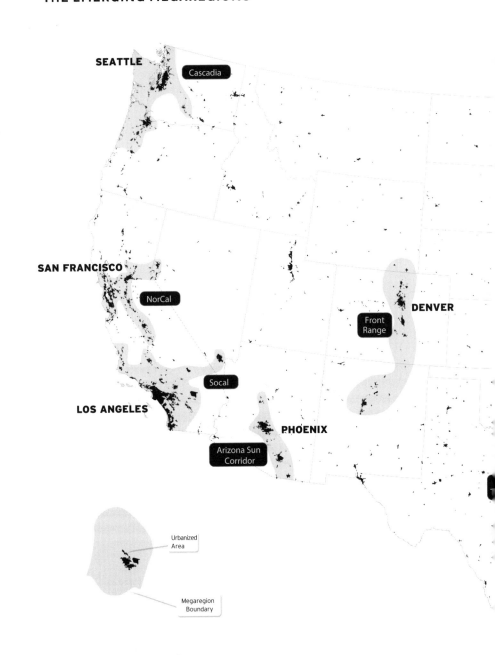

SEATTLE

Cascadia

SAN FRANCISCO

NorCal

DENVER

Front Range

Socal

LOS ANGELES

PHOENIX

Arizona Sun Corridor

Urbanized Area

Megaregion Boundary

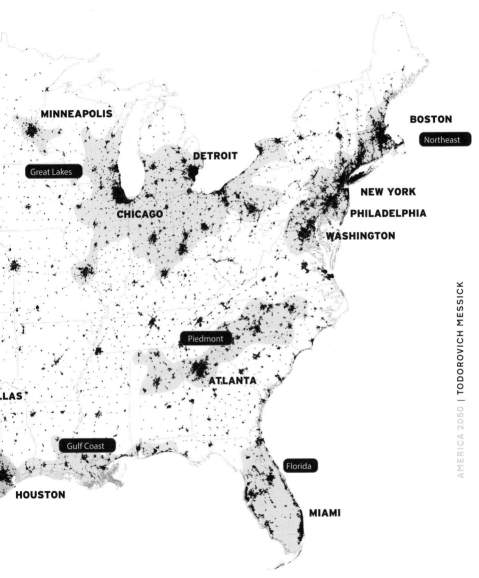

© REGIONAL PLAN ASSOCIATION

MINNEAPOLIS

BOSTON

Northeast

Great Lakes

DETROIT

CHICAGO

NEW YORK

PHILADELPHIA

WASHINGTON

Piedmont

ATLANTA

LAS

Gulf Coast

Florida

HOUSTON

MIAMI

AMERICA 2050 | TODOROVICH MESSICK

32

33

AMERICA 2050:
THE TRANS-AMERICAN PASSENGER NETWORK

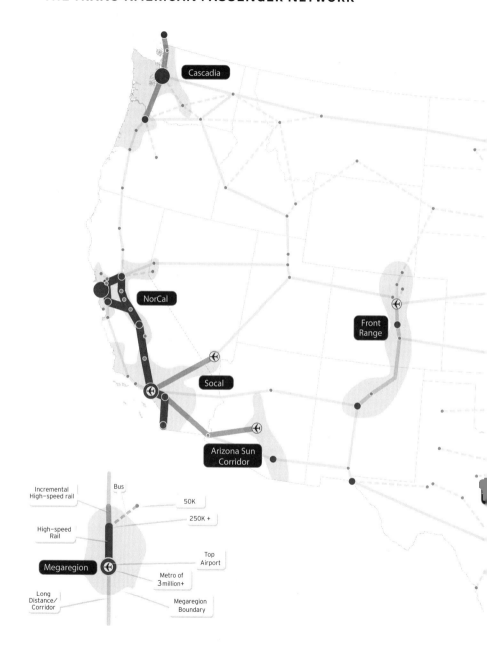

Cascadia

NorCal

Front Range

Socal

Arizona Sun Corridor

Incremental High-speed rail

Bus

50K

250K +

High-speed Rail

Top Airport

Megaregion

Metro of 3 million+

Long Distance/ Corridor

Megaregion Boundary

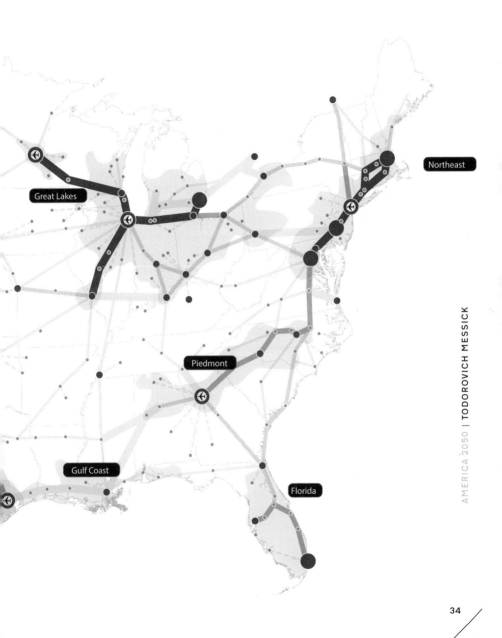

Northeast

Great Lakes

Piedmont

Gulf Coast

Florida

AMERICA 2050 | TODOROVICH MESSICK

SLOW INFRASTRUCTURE AND
THE EMERGING MEGAREGIONS

Cascadia

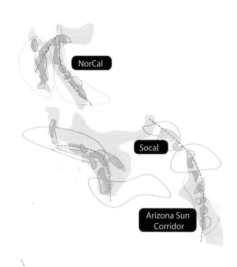

NorCal

Socal

Arizona Sun
Corridor

Front
Range

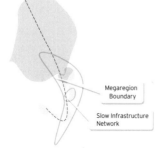

Megaregion
Boundary

Slow Infrastructure
Network

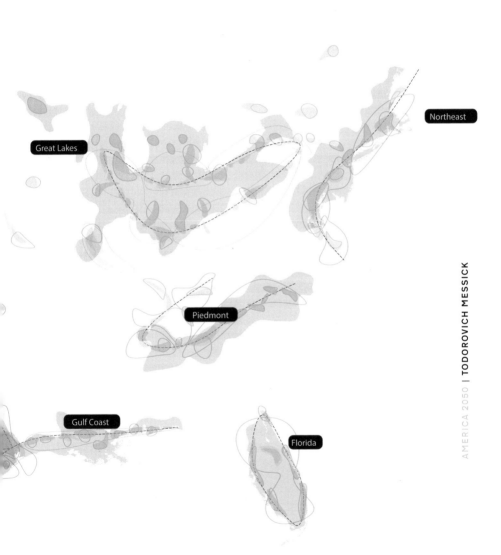

Northeast

Great Lakes

Piedmont

Gulf Coast

Florida

SLOW INFRASTRUCTURE AND
THE TRANS-AMERICAN NETWORK

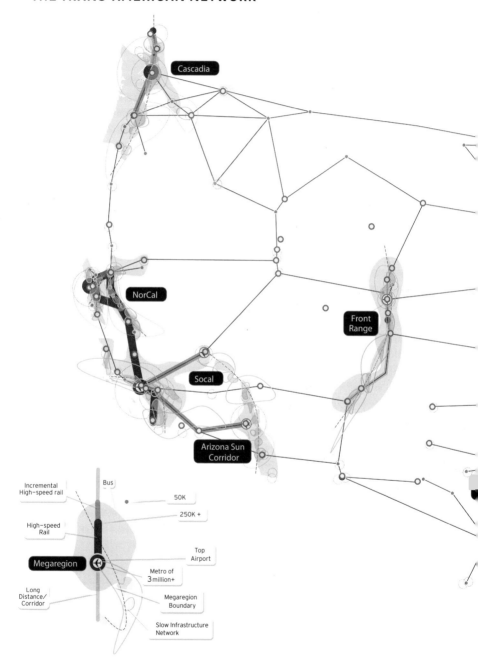

Cascadia

NorCal

Front Range

Socal

Arizona Sun Corridor

Incremental High-speed rail

Bus

50K

250K +

High-speed Rail

Top Airport

Megaregion

Metro of 3 million+

Long Distance/ Corridor

Megaregion Boundary

Slow Infrastructure Network

Great Lakes

Northeast

Piedmont

Gulf Coast

Florida

GARDEN [CITY] STATE

PHILIP TIDWELL

Cleared and drained, dredged and filled, divided and sold, New Jersey has developed rapidly over the last half-century. The decentralized urbanization of the state, undertaken with little comprehensive planning, is emblematic of late-twentieth century sprawl. The phrase "Garden State" is often seen as either a memory or a misnomer, but the label is less a myth than a testament to the complex identity of a place that is at once dense and dispersed. Many New Jersey residents are moving to smaller and more isolated communities, causing new housing and infrastructure to be placed immediately adjacent to verdant agricultural lands, dense pine forests, and long stretches of ocean shore. With nearly nine million residents on less than nine thousand square miles, New Jersey manages to be denser than any other state in the nation while boasting only one city with a population of more than a quarter-million (Newark). Today it may be more productive to think of New Jersey not as the densest state but rather as one of the most complicated, diverse, and expansive American cities.

Seen in this light, this unified but diverse urban agglomeration makes clear the intimate relationship between dispersion and mobility. As the state's sprawling growth has continued, so has its construction of new streets and roads. According to the New Jersey Bureau of Transportation Data Development, the state added more than 3,000 miles of road between 2001 and 2011, most to serve local pockets of urbanity. Today the state manages more than 39,000 miles of public roadway, and each year the cost to repair and maintain this network adds a significant burden to state and local governmental budgets. As energy costs rise along with the force and frequency of severe weather events, the resources required to fuel this auto-centric system are not likely to decrease.

At the same time, a burgeoning desire for digital connectivity is beginning to call this dependence on the automobile into question. Personal computing—both ubiquitous and incompatible with driving—has introduced a new cultural condition that provides an opportunity to challenge the primacy of the car. For this reason, and for many other reasons already identified by the Regional Plan Association, the development of faster rail service across the region is essential to New Jersey's future. But although high-speed passenger service promises to bring benefits to the state and its commuters, the full potential of these efforts will only be realized after they are integrated with existing patterns of urbanization. Rather than reinforcing an already problematic dependency on the automobile, investments in infrastructure should reclaim and reinvent existing systems by adapting them to new modes of mobility. The railroads, canals, and electrical grids that once supported rapid urbanization across the state have now become smaller, smarter, or in many cases made obsolete by new technology. Today these zones of abandoned infrastructure divide many towns and cities into fragmented neighborhoods. By recuperating the thousands of acres of undeveloped land on and adjacent to these pieces of infrastructure, the state has an opportunity to produce a new urban condition that could drive growth for a new century.

Garden [City] State proposes a transformation of these old and obsolete infrastructures into a new zone of slow infrastructure. The speculative project described throughout this atlas envisions a greenway, or continuous transportation loop, that will integrate public spaces with recreational areas and cultural facilities across the state. By introducing alternate modes of transit, its goal is to stitch together neighborhoods that have been separated from nearby town centers. Resources invested into the greenway would go toward encouraging density within existing urban areas rather than developing new areas of New Jersey's landscape. Taken as a whole, the project creates a blueprint for smart growth around the state.

The drawings and images presented here develop the basic diagram of this green loop of movement and recreation by delineating paths and conditions in twelve specific towns. Together they suggest a complex and varied urbanism composed of links between existing infrastructure and new mobility systems. The development of these drawings has depended not only on the information gleaned from existing town plans and geographic information systems but also on a careful analysis of aerial imagery. Although part of the representational and conceptual technology of urbanism since the nineteenth century, the aerial view has reemerged today as a tool of remarkable clarity and ubiquity. If, as architectural historian Anthony Vidler has suggested, this means of viewing the city once operated as a system of organization and control, it has served here as a means of circumventing those systems and of uncovering layers of inhabitation and use. No longer fixed in scale or position, today's satellite imagery allows us to scan an area or region and detect conditions we might otherwise overlook.

The vestiges of defunct infrastructure and industrial activity barely visible on New Jersey's land-use plans and transportation maps can be readily detected in satellite views. The high-voltage lines that cut across the state, for example, reveal a fascinating network of thoroughfares that deserve reconsideration. Such skeletal remains and subtle presences are easily obscured, erased, or ignored in contemporary data sets, but they remain starkly visible in the landscape. And so while the abandoned systems of infrastructure may have produced the state's current reserve of disjointed and undeveloped land, they have also provided us with an opportunity for future action. It is toward capitalizing on that opportunity that this speculative atlas is directed.

NEW JERSEY TOWNS

TOM WRIGHT

Among the states in the northeast, New Jersey is both unique and prototypical. The state contains more than five hundred cities and towns, all fiercely independent but shaped by common metropolitan, regional, and national trends. Bordering New York City and Philadelphia, it lies at the heart of the megaregion that extends from Boston to Washington, DC. Benjamin Franklin, whose estranged loyalist son was the last royal governor of New Jersey, famously called it a keg tapped at both ends. Yet for all its dysfunctionality, New Jersey remains a vibrant, prosperous state that has experienced enormous growth and prosperity in the past two decades

One-quarter of the state's northern residents now live within one mile of a train station and as a result, the state added five times more commuters to New York City in the last decade than did the suburbs of Connecticut, Long Island, and the Hudson Valley combined. As this growth continues over the coming decades, it is likely to occur in locations outside of the New Jersey's existing urban centers, placing new pressures on many small towns across the state. These pressures must be anticipated and directed in a way that conserves the essential character of these communities as well as the state's environmental resources. The towns selected here have been chosen as case studies for their likelihood of growth and their geographic importance. Located in the southern portion of the state and surrounding the sensitive Pine Barrens region, they outline an increasingly important area of development for the future of the state.

NEW BRUNSWICK AND PRINCETON

The "academic axis" between New Brunswick and Princeton stretches twenty miles along Route 1 and the Northeast Corridor Line to link New Jersey's premiere institutions of higher education—Rutgers and Princeton universities. New Brunswick, with its small-town charm, is the urban cousin to Princeton. It is the world headquarters of Johnson & Johnson and in some ways the urban, cultural, and political heart of the state. While New Jersey (and the nation) turned its back on cities such as Newark, Camden, Trenton, and Paterson after the riots of the 1960s, New Brunswick thrived as a sort of "middle-city" due to its smaller size, the loyalty of Rutgers alumni, and the extraordinary commitment of Johnson & Johnson. Over the past decade, a public/private development corporation has successfully redeveloped the downtown area, and the university continues to thrive.

While Rutgers focuses on its relationship with the state, Princeton more often casts its eyes farther afield—to New York City, Boston, and Washington, DC. In addition to a world-class university, the municipality shelters the Institute for Advanced Study (which hosted Albert Einstein from 1933 to 1955), the Princeton Theological Seminary, and other colleges and secondary schools, creating an "Athens of Mercer County" effect. The downtown suffered during the 1970s as Route 1 development threatened the vitality of the area, but it has rebounded strongly during the past quarter-century. As of 2013 Princeton Borough and Princeton Township have consolidated as a single administrative entity.

FLORENCE-ROEBLING

Florence-Roebling is positioned midway between Trenton and Philadelphia on the banks of the Delaware River and nested within the larger township of Florence at the heart of Burlington County and the agricultural center of the state. Although the county is predominantly agricultural in character, the area along the banks of the river is mostly urban and populated with numerous bedroom communities that are home to state office workers, who commute to the nearby capital via light rail on New Jersey Transit's *River Line*. Though they were counted as two separate 'census-designated places' in 2010, Florence and Roebling have usually been considered as a single unit and have been treated here as a combined entity.

The village of Roebling, an industrial community from the turn of the century, is a jewel of early 20th century town planning. Constructed between 1904 and 1921 on a former peach and potato farm, Charles G. Roebling was responsible for the design of the community which he founded together with his brother Washington A. Roebling. Both men were sons of the renowned engineer John A. Roebling who was responsible for the design of the Brooklyn Bridge (1867–83) as well as numerous other steel structures across the country. The steel mill and wire rope factory that served as the industrial center of this company town produce cable for projects ranging from the Golden Gate Bridge (1933-37) to the elevators of the Empire State Building (1929-31). In 1982 the Environmental Protection agency designated the Roebling Steel Co. site as a 200-acre superfund site with 70 buildings in need of rehabilitation or destruction. This area was selected for investigation in light of its industrial and urban history as well as its location in Burlington County.

CHERRY HILL

The sprawling Philadelphia suburb of Cherry Hill is located just east of the Delaware River in Camden County. The city, with its wealthy and predominantly white population, is seven miles southeast of Camden, the poor and predominantly African American county seat—an adjacency that speaks to the economic and racial segregation of the many post-war suburbs.

Despite its proximity to Philadelphia and Camden, which are both served by numerous regional and state railway networks, the community is completely car dependent and relies on a few state highways that cut through the township. Cherry Hill is an in-between place, which succeeded from the 1970s to the 1990s by isolating itself from its immediate neighbors but its growth has slowed dramatically since 2000. Today it finds itself unable to wall off adjacent communities or their troubles and has struggled to maintain its individual character. For a prosperous future, Cherry Hill will need to become something other than a suburban enclave.

HAMMONTON

The Atlantic County town of Hammonton is situated between Philadelphia and Atlantic City in the southern section of the New Jersey Pine Barrens. This heavily forested coastal plain was famously celebrated by John McPhee in his 1968 classic *The Pine Barrens* for its distinctive geography—fostered by porous, sandy soil—and for the culture of its native population, referred to as "pineys." Rural, agricultural, sprawling, and flat, Hammonton is located entirely within the Pine Barrens and has built on its agricultural identity by proclaiming itself the "blueberry capital of the world". For the last ten years it has enjoyed robust growth by focusing on its quality of life and small-town scale. But as the economic strength of Atlantic City falters, and southern New Jersey debates what kind of region it wants to become, Hammonton faces important decisions about its growth and development in relation to the region.

ATLANTIC CITY

Atlantic City is the capital of southern and coastal New Jersey. After the state legalized gambling in 1976, the nineteenth-century seaside resort grew into the largest tourism and gambling destination in the eastern United States. In recent decades the city has seen its fortunes ebb and flow, as gaming opportunities in surrounding states have expanded. To determine what the "next" Atlantic City will be, Governor Chris Christie created a commission in 2010 to focus state initiatives and energy on revitalizing the downtown area. In 2013 he directed the Port Authority of New York & New Jersey to take over the local airport—an extraordinary expansion of the authority's geographical scope.

The extensive tourism and leisure industry in Atlantic City make it unique within the state (which otherwise lacks such amenities) and one of southern New Jersey's greatest economic generators. In some sense, Atlantic City is almost outside New Jersey, in the way that New York and Philadelphia similarly stand independent of their respective states.

TOMS RIVER

A sprawling suburban community, Toms River is a replica of Cherry Hill transplanted to the Atlantic shore. Located in Ocean County, New Jersey's fastest growing county for the last two decades, the township has expanded along a north-south axis on the eastern seaboard. This model of growth resembles that which was prominent in the 1980s, particularly as the homes that comprise the suburb are often large, with garages and basement movie theaters as primary attractors. Its barrier peninsula is characterized by cultural and economic segregation: poor and rich areas are in close proximity but unseen barriers keep outsiders away.

Toms River was severely affected by the damage brought by Hurricane Sandy in October 2012. Many low-lying areas of the township saw their worst flooding ever and the barrier islands, just across the bridge, suffered even worse devastation from the storm surge brought by the Hurricane. As most other towns on the shore Toms River will have to plan for a radically different pattern of growth in the future.

POINT PLEASANT

Water forms the life blood of Point Pleasant Borough. Almost twenty miles of shoreline, including numerous lagoons, encompass the borders of the town. The Manasquan River to the north and Bay Head Harbor to the south and east are connected by a canal that bisects the community, connecting these two bodies of water. Along the shore Point Pleasant Beach juts out into the Atlantic Ocean.

While the tourists that come to the area—mostly New Jersey natives—travel through the town to access and enjoy the shore, the residents, as in most New Jersey towns, face a future of drinking water scarcity. The three aquifers, Kirkwood, Englishtown, and Raritan-Magothy that supply Point Pleasant with its potable drinking water receive their rainwater for recharging from the shrinking territory out of the town, while the storm water that flows off an increasingly developed landscape of sprawl ends up dumped into the tidal waters and wasted.

RED BANK

Red Bank is situated along the Navesink River in Middlesex County and connected to the Atlantic Ocean via the Sandy Hook bay. Due to its elevation and position along a sheltered inland waterway, the city has been spared the most dramatic effects of coastal flooding while benefitting from close links to New York City by ferry as well as freeways and the North Jersey Coast Line. Originally developed as commercial and manufacturing center, this port town once shipped people and goods to New York City but has been reinvented during recent decades as a complete community which acts as a center of business and commerce for the northern coast of the state.

KEYPORT

The Monmouth county community of Keyport is situated along the Raritan Bay adjacent to an inland waterway and Keyport Harbor. Once known for its thriving oyster production, the shellfish industry in the area has all but disappeared in recent decades due to overfishing and industrial pollution. Today the town has joined with other municipalities in the area in an effort to develop economic growth based on the beauty of the coastal landscape and its maritime history. But unlike the towns along the southern shore, residents and visitors to Keyport and the other Raritan Bay shore communities are more closely linked to New York City by ferries, freeways and the North Jersey Coast Line.

SOUTH AMBOY AND SAYREVILLE

South Amboy and Sayreville are commuter towns located at the mouth of the Raritan River and separated by the Garden State Parkway. These former industrial towns have been developing in very different directions.

The much larger borough of Sayerville located on the Raritan River near the Raritan Bay, was and remains an industrial town that is being modernized with the addition of new technology companies. Construction started this year to implement a new master plan that will create a mixed use development which includes a shopping center, apartments, town homes, offices, and multiple marinas.

Sayerville recently suffered extensive flooding near the river during Hurricane Sandy and was offered by the federal government to buyout 250 houses in the floodplain near the river which was accepted by many residents setting up a precedent for a future sustainable management of the New Jersey Shore.

South Amboy has both embraced its past when the city's economy was based on shipping and manufacturing but also looking into a sustainable future by developing a master plan for a greenway, restoring the storefronts and promoting transit oriented residential development in the downtown area adjacent to the train station. And, as always, the rail line is key. The train which is now solely in a line for commuters to New York City is the centerpiece of an envisioned transportation hub that would also incorporate buses and maybe a ferry, coming full circle to South Amboy's beginnings.

A SPECULATIVE ATLAS

MATTHEW CLARKE
WILLEM BONING
PHOEBE SPRINGSTUBB
SAM STEWART-HALEVY
PHILIP TIDWELL
STEPHANIE LEE
CONG WANG
LYDIA XYNOGALA

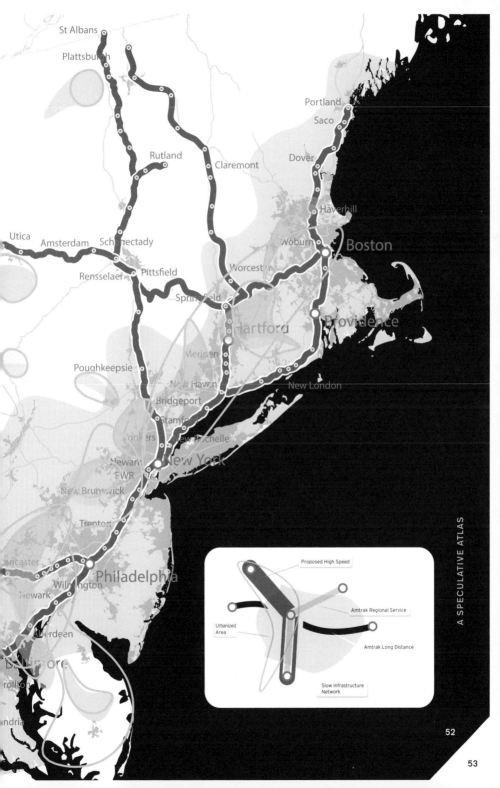

St Albans

Plattsburgh

Rutland

Claremont

Portland

Saco

Dover

Haverhill

Utica

Amsterdam   Schenectady

Rensselaer   Pittsfield

Springfield

Woburn   Boston

Worcester

Poughkeepsie

Hartford   Providence

Meriden

New Haven   New London

Bridgeport

Stamford

Yonkers   New Rochelle

Newark   New York

EWR

New Brunswick

Trenton

Lancaster

Wilmington   Philadelphia

Newark

Aberdeen

Baltimore

Carrollton

Alexandria

Proposed High Speed

Amtrak Regional Service

Urbanized
Area

Amtrak Long Distance

Slow Infrastructure
Network

GROWTH BY METRO AREA

Taken as a whole the growth rate of New Jersey's population now exceeds that of New York City, Philadelphia and even heavily urbanized corridor of I-95 which cuts across the state. New Jersey today is a veritable city-state poised to grow further in the coming decade, but where will the new residents go, and how will an auto-centric infrastructure keep them moving?

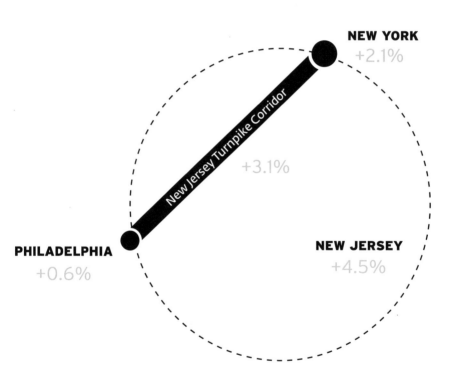

NEW YORK
+2.1%

New Jersey Turnpike Corridor
+3.1%

PHILADELPHIA
+0.6%

NEW JERSEY
+4.5%

*SOURCE: U.S. CENSUS BUREAU 2000 AND 2010 DATA REPORTS.

20%	■
10% to 20%	■
0% to 10%	■
0% to -10%	■
-10% to -20.0%	■
-20% or more	□

TRIANGULATING GROWTH

Development in the state has been driven primarily by automobile-based transportation between the *extra muros* poles of Philadelphia and New York City. Introducing Atlantic City as the third point of the triangle creates a new loop of infrastructure. The Garden State Parkway, the New Jersey Turnpike, and the Atlantic City Expressway will become high-speed-transit corridors.

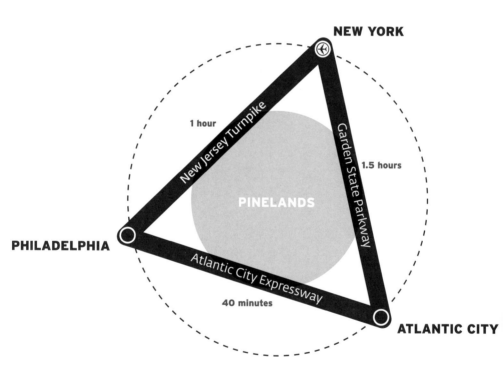

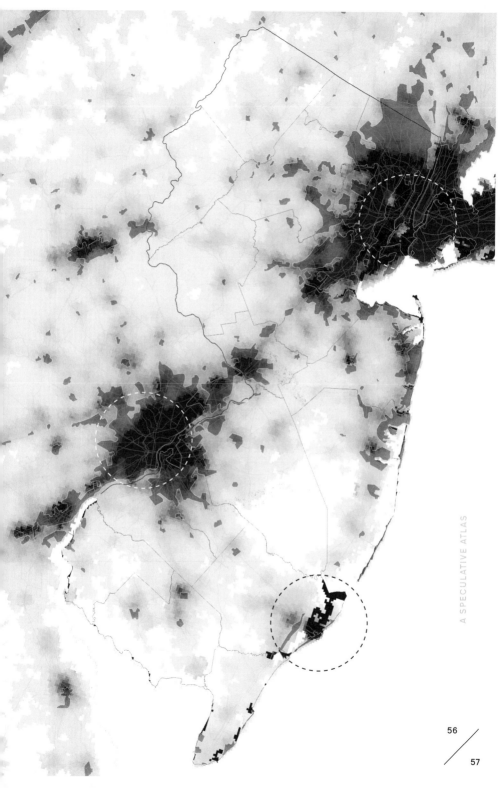

IDENTIFYING CENTERS OF GROWTH

In order to test and develop the green-loop strategies explored at the national scale, we have identified twelve centers of growth that are expected to increase in population during the coming decade.

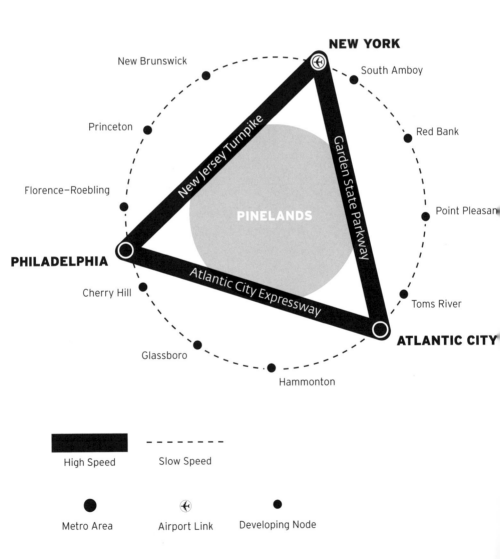

NEW YORK

New Brunswick

South Amboy

Princeton

Red Bank

Florence/Roebling

Point Pleasant

PHILADELPHIA

Toms River

Cherry Hill

Glassboro

Hammonton

ATLANTIC CITY

CONNECTING TO THE REGION

The loop proposal breaks down into four distinct sections: an industrial northern section on the Raritan Bay coastline including Sayreville, South Amboy and Keyport, a western section from New Brunswick to Florence-Roebling, a southern section between Cherry Hill and Atlantic City, and an eastern coastal segment from Toms River to Red Bank. Splitting the loop into sections allows for development of specific conditions that call for different interventions across the state.

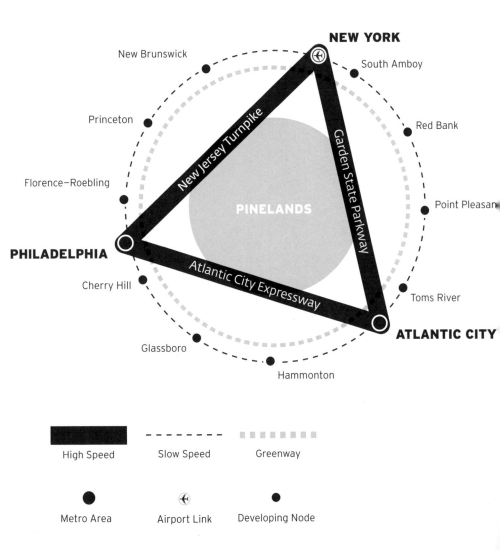

PROMOTING STRATEGIC DENSITY

It does not always make sense to promote growth, so the strategy has been to identify what already exists—existing hard lines of infrastructure, such as highways and railways—and then to work within the leftover spaces, reclaiming abandoned or underutilized corridors and introducing different scales of movement, biking, walking, running, car sharing, commuting etc., to join these hard lines.

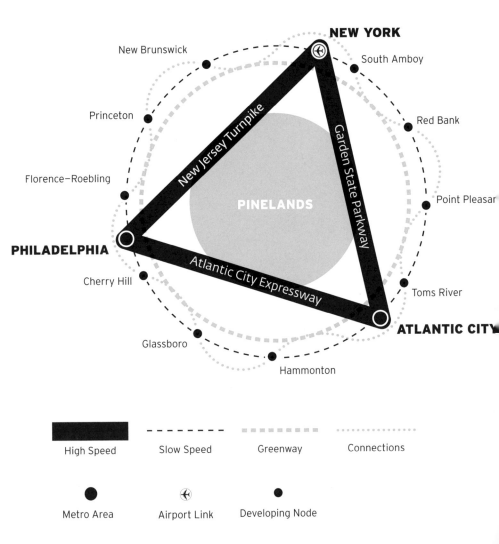

PINELANDS
CONSERVATION
AREA

HIGHLANDS

PRINCET

FLORENCE-ROEBLING

1 MILE

5 MILES

NEW BRUNSWICK

SOUTH AMBOY

PINELANDS

64

A SPECULATIVE ATLAS | NEW BRUNSWICK

RUTGER'S ECOLOGICAL PRESERVE

JOHNSON AND JOHNSON

BUCCLEUCH PARK

RUTGERS

CHILDREN'S HOSPITAL

NEW BRUNSWICK AMTRAK STATION

ST PETER THE APOSTLE
ELEMENTARY SCHOOL
CANCER INSTITUTE OF NEW JERSEY
CHILDREN'S SPECIALIZED HOSPITAL
MIDDLESEX SUPERIOR COURT

INSTITUTE FOR HEALTH SCIENCES

DONALDSON COUNTY PARK

JOYCE KIMMER PARK

JERSEY AVE

NEW BRUNSWICK MIDDLE SCHOOL

BAKER PARK
RUTGERS UNIVERSITY DOUGLASS CAMPUS
ELMWOOD CEMETARY

BABBAGE PARK
VAN LIEW CEMETARY

1/16

1/4 MILE

AREA
5.789 MI² (14.995 KM²)
5.227 MI² (13.539 KM²) LAND
0.562 MI² (1.456 KM²) (9.71%) WATER

POPULATION
55,181 PEOPLE
14,119 HOUSEHOLDS
 7,751 FAMILIES

POPULATION DENSITY
10,556.4/MI² (4,075.8/KM²)
15,053 HOUSING UNITS AT AN AVERAGE DENSITY OF 2,879.7/MI²
    (1,111.9/KM²)

45.43% (25,071) WHITE
16.04% (8,852) BLACK OR AFRICAN AMERICAN
 0.90% (498)   AMERICAN INDIAN AND ALASKA NATIVE
 7.60% (4,195) ASIAN
 0.03% (19)   NATIVE HAWAIIAN AND OTHER PACIFIC ISLANDER
49.93% (27,553) HISPANIC OR LATINO (OF ANY RACE)
 4.39% (2,424) TWO OR MORE RACES
25.59% (14,122) SOME OTHER RACE

COMMUNITY
PARK NORTH

N. HARISSON ST.

JOHN WITHERSPOON
MIDDLE SCHOOL

WITHERSPOON
STREET

PRINCETON
CEMETERY

ST PAULS
ROMAN
CATHOLIC
CHURCH

NASSAU STREET

WITHERSPOON
SQUARE

PALMER
SQUARE

EPISCOPAL
CHURCH

PRINCETON UNIVERSITY CAMPUS

N. HARISSEN CT.

PRINCETON DINKY
STATION

MARQUAND PARK

RARITAN CANAL

SPRINGDALE GOLF CLUB

PRINCETON RAILROAD

ALEXANDER ROAD

1/16

1/4 MILE

AREA
18.363 MI² (47.56 KM²)
17.933 MI² (46.45 KM²) LAND
 0.430 MI² (1.11 KM²) (2.34%) WATER

POPULATION
28,572 PEOPLE
 9,521 HOUSEHOLDS
 5,968 FAMILIES

POPULATION DENSITY
1600.0/MI² (600.0/KM²)
10,302 HOUSING UNITS AT AN AVERAGE DENSITY OF 574.5/MI² (221.8/KM²)

76.83% (21,953) WHITE
 6.50% (1,857) BLACK OR AFRICAN AMERICAN
 0.61% (175)   AMERICAN INDIAN AND ALASKA NATIVE
15.72% (4,491) ASIAN
 0.17% (48)   NATIVE HAWAIIAN AND OTHER PACIFIC ISLANDER
 8.37% (2,392) HISPANIC OR LATINO (OF ANY RACE)
 3.16% (904)   TWO OR MORE RACES
 3.57% (1,019) SOME OTHER RACE

STEEL FACTORIES

H. KENNETH
WILKIE PARK

VOLUNTEER'S
PARK

FLORENCE
WATERFRONT
SCHOOL

RECREATION
COMPLEX

RIVER'S EDGE DEVEL

ROEBLING PARK

ROEBLING
MUSEUM

NYIKITA FIELD

FLORENCE
TOWNSHIP
PUBLIC LIBRARY

FLORENCE
SCHOOL
DISTRICT

EXISTING RAIL

FLORENCE TRAIN
STATION

1/16

1/4 MILE

AREA
2.663 MI² (6.893 KM²)
2.271 MI² (5.880 KM²) LAND
0.392 MI² (1.013 KM²) (14.72%) WATER

POPULATION
8,141 PEOPLE
3,267 HOUSEHOLDS
2,131 FAMILIES

POPULATION DENSITY
3584.8/MI² (1384.5/KM²)
3,479 HOUSING UNITS AT AN AVERAGE DENSITY OF 1531.9/MI² (591.7/KM²)

80.09% (6520)	WHITE
14.49% (1180)	BLACK OR AFRICAN AMERICAN
0.71% (58)	AMERICAN INDIAN AND ALASKA NATIVE
4.25% (346)	ASIAN
0.06% (5)	NATIVE HAWAIIAN AND OTHER PACIFIC ISLANDER
5.01% (408)	HISPANIC OR LATINO (OF ANY RACE)
3.57% (291)	TWO OR MORE RACES
1.57% (128)	SOME OTHER RACE

CHERRY HILL

GLASSBORO

1 MILE

5 MILES

PINELANDS

NEW JERSEY TRANSIT RAIL

CITY EXPRESSWAY

ATLANTIC CITY

82

KING HIGHWAY SOUTH

HIGHWAY 295

STRIP MALL

MARITON PIKE

STRIP MALL

BRACE ROAD

HIGHWAY 295

NEW JERSEY TURNPIKE

HIGHWAY 295

1/16

1/4 MILE

AREA
24.244 MI² (62.792 KM²)
24.097 MI² (62.410 KM²) LAND
 0.147 MI² (0.382 KM²) 0.61% WATER

POPULATION
71,045 PEOPLE
26,882 HOUSEHOLDS
19,301 FAMILIES

POPULATION DENSITY
2948.3/MI² (1138.3/KM²)
28,452 HOUSING UNITS AT AN AVERAGE DENSITY OF 1,180.7/MI² (455.9/KM²)

78.06%	(55,459)	WHITE
6.14%	(4,360)	BLACK OR AFRICAN AMERICAN
0.11%	(78)	AMERICAN INDIAN AND ALASKA NATIVE
11.69%	(8,304)	ASIAN
0.02%	(13)	NATIVE HAWAIIAN AND OTHER PACIFIC ISLANDER
5.64%	(4,007)	HISPANIC OR LATINO (OF ANY RACE)
2.15%	(1,529)	TWO OR MORE RACES
1.83%	(1,302)	SOME OTHER RACE

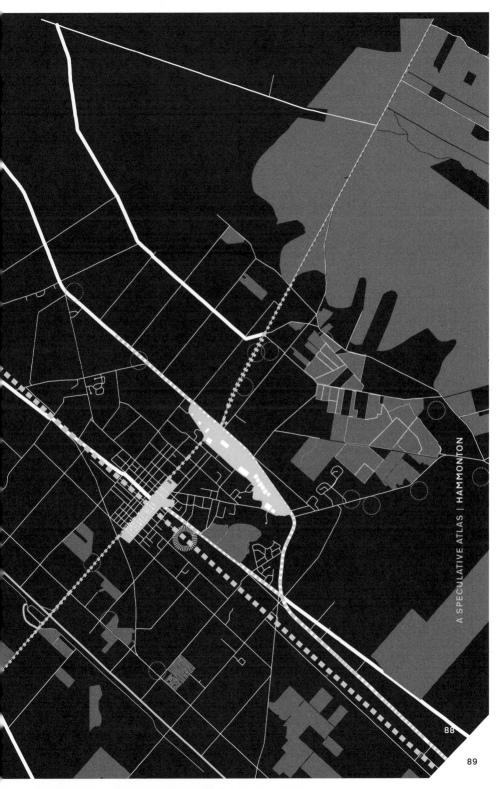

88

PINELAND FOREST

BIKE PATH

PROTECTED FARMLAND

STRIP MALL

MAIN STREET
RETAIL AND
ARTS DISTRICT

HAMMONTON TRAIN STATION

BIKE PATH

PROTECTED FARMLAND

1/16

1/4 MILE

ATLANTIC CITY
EXPRESSWAY

AREA
41.419 MI² (107.274 KM²)
40.887 MI² (105.897 KM²) LAND
 0.532 MI² (1.377 KM²) (1.28%) WATER

POPULATION
14,791 PEOPLE
 5,408 HOUSEHOLDS
 3,759 FAMILIES

POPULATION DENSITY
361.8/MI² (139.7/KM²)
5,715 HOUSING UNITS AT AN AVERAGE DENSITY OF 139.8/MI² (54.0 /KM²)

81.67% (12,080) WHITE
 3.00% (444)   BLACK OR AFRICAN AMERICAN
 0.28% (42)   AMERICAN INDIAN AND ALASKA NATIVE
 1.37% (203)   ASIAN
 0.01% (2)   NATIVE HAWAIIAN AND OTHER PACIFIC ISLANDER
20.93% (3,096) HISPANIC OR LATINO (OF ANY RACE)
 2.85% (421)   TWO OR MORE RACES
10.81% (1,599) SOME OTHER RACE

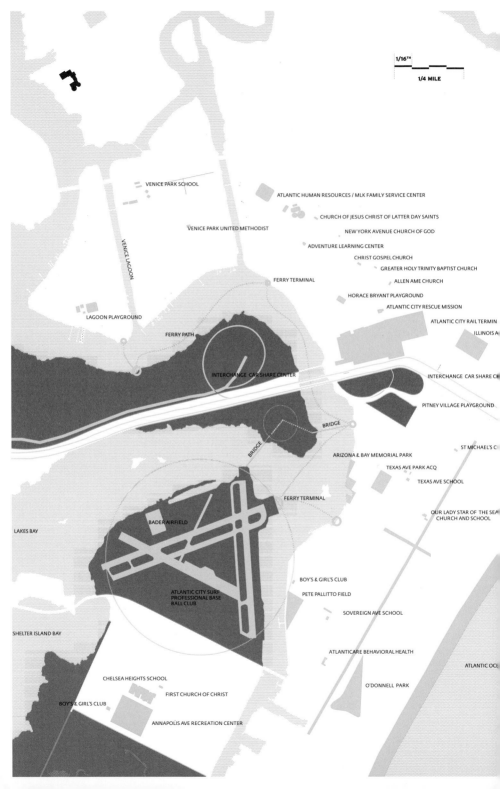

1/16 TH

1/4 MILE

VENICE PARK SCHOOL

ATLANTIC HUMAN RESOURCES / MLK FAMILY SERVICE CENTER

CHURCH OF JESUS CHRIST OF LATTER DAY SAINTS

VENICE PARK UNITED METHODIST

NEW YORK AVENUE CHURCH OF GOD

ADVENTURE LEARNING CENTER

CHRIST GOSPEL CHURCH

GREATER HOLY TRINITY BAPTIST CHURCH

VENICE LAGOON

FERRY TERMINAL

ALLEN AME CHURCH

HORACE BRYANT PLAYGROUND

ATLANTIC CITY RESCUE MISSION

LAGOON PLAYGROUND

ATLANTIC CITY RAIL TERMIN

ILLINOIS A

FERRY PATH

INTERCHANGE CAR SHARE CENTER

INTERCHANGE CAR SHARE C

PITNEY VILLAGE PLAYGROUND

BRIDGE

BRIDGE

ST MICHAEL'S C

ARIZONA & BAY MEMORIAL PARK

TEXAS AVE PARK ACQ

TEXAS AVE SCHOOL

FERRY TERMINAL

OUR LADY STAR OF THE SEA
CHURCH AND SCHOOL

LAKES BAY

BADER AIRFIELD

BOY'S & GIRL'S CLUB

PETE PALLITTO FIELD

ATLANTIC CITY SURF
PROFESSIONAL BASE
BALL CLUB

SOVEREIGN AVE SCHOOL

SHELTER ISLAND BAY

ATLANTICARE BEHAVIORAL HEALTH

ATLANTIC OCE

CHELSEA HEIGHTS SCHOOL

O'DONNELL PARK

FIRST CHURCH OF CHRIST

BOY'S & GIRL'S CLUB

ANNAPOLIS AVE RECREATION CENTER

AREA
17.037 MI² (44.125 KM²)
10.747 MI² (27.835 KM²) LAND
 6.290 MI² (16.290 KM²) (36.92%) WATER

POPULATION
39,558 PEOPLE
15,504 HOUSEHOLDS
 8,558 FAMILIES

POPULATION DENSITY
3,680.8/MI² (1,421.2/KM²)
20,013 HOUSING UNITS AT AN AVERAGE DENSITY OF 1,862.2/MI² (719.0/KM²)

26.65% (10,543) WHITE
38.29% (15,148) BLACK OR AFRICAN AMERICAN
 0.61% (242)   AMERICAN INDIAN AND ALASKA NATIVE
 5.55% (6,153) ASIAN
 0.05% (18)   NATIVE HAWAIIAN AND OTHER PACIFIC ISLANDER
30.45% (12,044) HISPANIC OR LATINO (OF ANY RACE)
 4.82% (1,905) TWO OR MORE RACES
14.03% (5,549) SOME OTHER RACE

A SPECULATIVE ATLAS | ATLANTIC CITY

1 MILE

5 MILES

WINDING RIVER PARK

SAINT JOSEPH
GRADE SCHOOL

TOMS RIVER HIGH
SCHOOL

OCEAN COUNTY
COURT
INFORMATION

CITY HALL

OCEAN COUNTY COURT
HOUSE

POST OFFICE

TOMS RIVER LIBRARY

HUDDY PARK

MATHIS PLAZA

CEDAR POINT

SOUTH TOMS RIVER PARK

1/16

1/4 MILE

AREA

52.884 MI² (136.969 KM²)
40.488 MI² (104.863 KM²) LAND
12.396 MI² (32.105 KM²) (23.44%) WATER

POPULATION

91,239 PEOPLE
34,760 HOUSEHOLDS
24,367 FAMILIES

POPULATION DENSITY

2,253.5/MI² (870.1/KM²)
43,334 HOUSING UNITS AT AN AVERAGE DENSITY OF 1,070.3/MI² (413.2/KM²)

89.91% (82,035) WHITE
 2.70% (2,465) BLACK OR AFRICAN AMERICAN
 0.17% (156)   AMERICAN INDIAN AND ALASKA NATIVE
 3.58% (3,266) ASIAN
 0.02% (17)   NATIVE HAWAIIAN AND OTHER PACIFIC ISLANDER
 7.93% (7,231) HISPANIC OR LATINO (OF ANY RACE)
 1.66% (1,515) TWO OR MORE RACES
 1.96% (1,785) SOME OTHER RACE

GULL ISLAND

BROAD AVE

POINT PLEASA
BEACH

LAKE LOUISE

G. HAROLD ANTRIM ELEMENTARY
SCHOOL

POINT PLEASANT TRAIN STOP

LITTLE SILVER LAKE

ARNOLD AVE

PLEASURE PARK

ST. PETER'S SCHOOL

POINT PLEASANT BEACH HIGH
SCHOOL

BOROUGH OF POINT PLEASANT
BEACH

BAY AVE

RICHMOND AVE

HAWTHORNE AVE

LAKE OF THE LILLIES

NURSERY SCHOOL

OCEAN ROAD

BIRD
SANCTUARY

SEA AVE

1/16

1/4 MILE

BAY HEAD TRAIN STOP

AREA
4.167 MI² (10.790 KM²)
3.489 MI² (9.035 KM²) LAND
0.678 MI² (1.755 KM²) (16.26%) WATER

POPULATION
18,392 PEOPLE
 7,273 HOUSEHOLDS
 4,982 FAMILIES

POPULATION DENSITY
5,272.1/MI² (2,035.6/KM²)
8,331 HOUSING UNITS AT AN AVERAGE DENSITY OF 2,388.1/MI² (922.1/KM²)

96.05% (17,666) WHITE
 0.41% (75)   BLACK OR AFRICAN AMERICAN
 0.13% (24)   AMERICAN INDIAN AND ALASKA NATIVE
 0.72% (133)   ASIAN
 0.03% (6)   NATIVE HAWAIIAN AND OTHER PACIFIC ISLANDER
 5.08% (935)   HISPANIC OR LATINO (OF ANY RACE)
 0.99% (183)   TWO OR MORE RACES
 1.66% (305)   SOME OTHER RACE

108

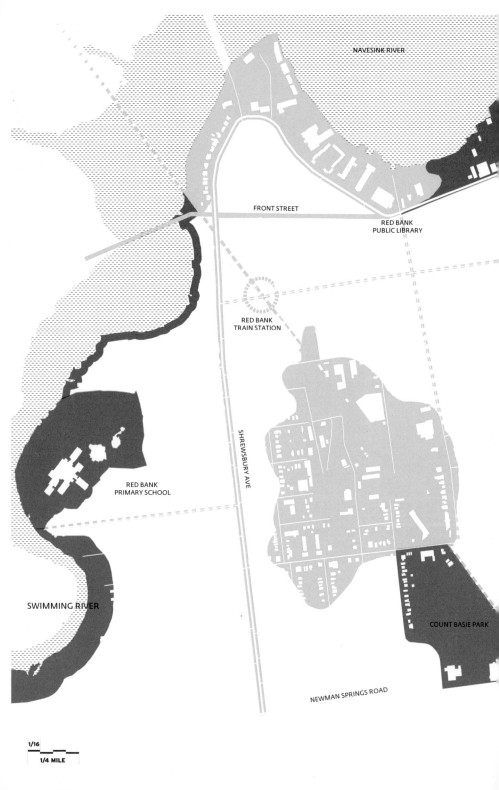

NAVESINK RIVER

FRONT STREET

RED BANK
PUBLIC LIBRARY

RED BANK
TRAIN STATION

SHREWSBURY AVE

RED BANK
PRIMARY SCHOOL

SWIMMING RIVER

COUNT BASIE PARK

NEWMAN SPRINGS ROAD

1/16
1/4 MILE

AREA
2.162 MI² (5.600 KM²)
1.739 MI² (4.504 KM²2) LAND
0.423 MI² (1.096 KM²) (19.58%) WATER

POPULATION
12,206 PEOPLE
 4,929 HOUSEHOLDS
 2,469 FAMILIES

POPULATION DENSITY
7,019.1/MI² (2,710.1/KM²)
5,381 HOUSING UNITS AT AN AVERAGE DENSITY OF 3,094.4/MI² (1,194.8/KM²)

63.20% (7,714)   WHITE
12.42% (1,516)   BLACK OR AFRICAN AMERICAN
 0.97% (118)   AMERICAN INDIAN AND ALASKA NATIVE
 1.85% (226)   ASIAN
 0.11% (13)   NATIVE HAWAIIAN AND OTHER PACIFIC ISLANDER
34.39% (4,198)   HISPANIC OR LATINO (OF ANY RACE)
 2.90% (354)   TWO OR MORE RACES
18.56% (2,265)   SOME OTHER RACE

HIGH-VOLTAGE LINE

GARDEN STATE PARKWAY

CSAO FREIGHT RAIL

CSAO FREIGHT RAIL

CHEES
STATE P

1 MILE

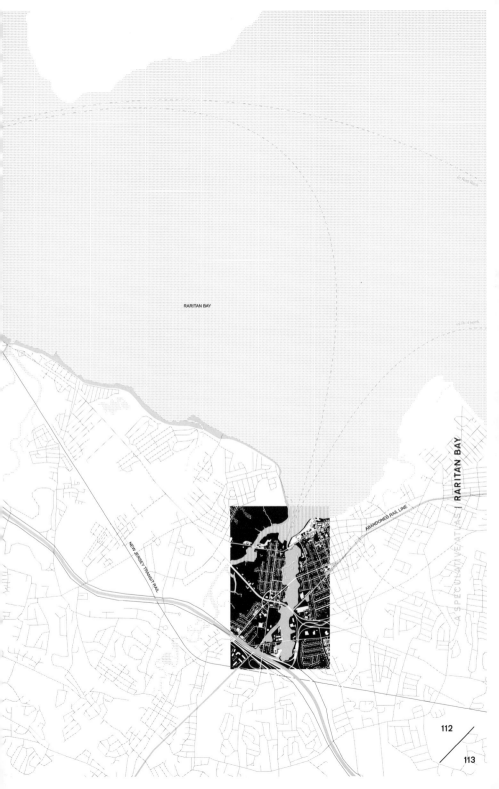

RARITAN BAY

NEW JERSEY TRANSIT RAIL

ABANDONED RAIL LINE

A SPECULATIVE ATLAS | RARITAN BAY

POWER
PLANT

SENIOR CITIZEN
CLUB

HIGH VOLTAGE
POWER LINE

HIGH VOLTAGE
POWER LINE

GREEN LOOP

URBAN LOOP

1/16TH

1/4 MILE

AREA
18.704 MI² (48.442 KM²)
15.842 MI² (41.030 KM²) LAND
 2.862 MI² (7.412 KM²) (15.30%) WATER

POPULATION
42,740 PEOPLE
15,636 HOUSEHOLDS
11,411 FAMILIES

POPULATION DENSITY
2,695.7/MI² (1,040.8/KM²)
16,393 HOUSING UNITS AT AN AVERAGE DENSITY OF 1,034.7/MI² (399.5/KM²)

68.60% (29,300) WHITE
11.60% (4,937) BLACK OR AFRICAN AMERICAN
 0.50% (211) AMERICAN INDIAN AND ALASKA NATIVE
17.10% (7,311) ASIAN
 0.20% (66) NATIVE HAWAIIAN AND OTHER PACIFIC ISLANDER
12.30% (5258) HISPANIC OR LATINO (OF ANY RACE)
 2.40% (1006) TWO OR MORE RACES
 4.60% (1,944) SOME OTHER RACE

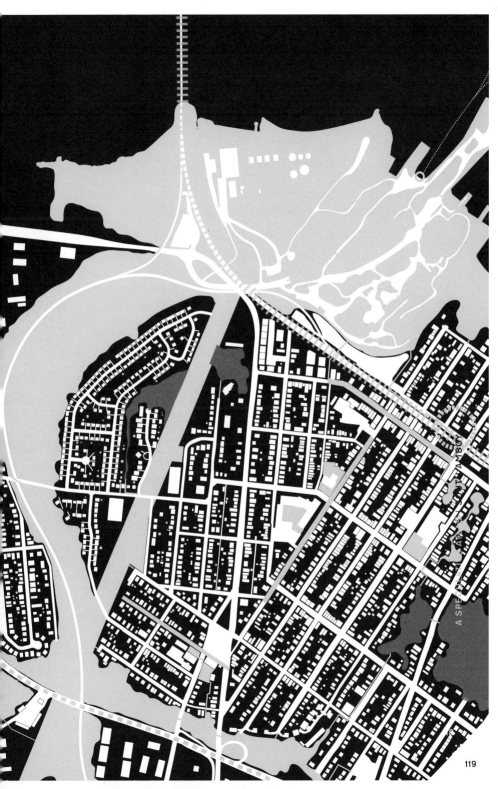

1/16TH

1/4 MILE

DEFUNCT
RAIL YARDS

HIGH VOLTAGE
POWER LINE

ST. MARY'S CHURCH

ST. MARY'S SCHOOL

SOUTH AMBOY TRA

GREEN LOOP

SOUTH AMBOY
SCHOOL

PINE AVENUE
PARK

SACRED HEART
CHURCH

SACRED HEART
SCHOOL

AREA
2.694 MI² (6.976 KM²)
1.548 MI² (4.008 KM²) LAND
1.146 MI² (2.967 KM²) (42.54%) WATER

POPULATION
8,631 PEOPLE
3,372 HOUSEHOLDS
2,256 FAMILIES

POPULATION DENSITY
5,577.1/MI² (2,153.3/KM²)
3,576 HOUSING UNITS AT AN AVERAGE DENSITY OF 2,310.7/MI² (892.2/KM²)

86.42% (7,459)	WHITE
4.43% (382)	BLACK OR AFRICAN AMERICAN
0.10% (9)	AMERICAN INDIAN AND ALASKA NATIVE
4.03% (348)	ASIAN
0.00% (0)	NATIVE HAWAIIAN AND OTHER PACIFIC ISLANDER
13.42% (1,158)	HISPANIC OR LATINO (OF ANY RACE)
2.03% (175)	TWO OR MORE RACES
2.99% (258)	SOME OTHER RACE

1 MILE

KEYPORT HARBOR

MARSH

HENRY HUDSON BIKE TRAIL

BASEBALL
DIAMONDS

GARDEN STATE PARKWAY

AREA
1.469 MI² (3.807 KM²)
1.395 MI² (3.614 KM²) LAND
0.074 MI² (0.193 KM²) (5.06%) WATER

POPULATION
7,240 PEOPLE
3,067 HOUSEHOLDS
1,694 FAMILIES

POPULATION DENSITY
5188.4/MI² (2003.3/KM²)
3,272 HOUSING UNITS AT AN AVERAGE DENSITY OF 2345.5/MI² (859.5/KM²)

82.00%	(5,940)	WHITE
8.20%	(596)	BLACK OR AFRICAN AMERICAN
0.90%	(66)	AMERICAN INDIAN AND ALASKA NATIVE
2.90%	(213)	ASIAN
0.10%	(10)	NATIVE HAWAIIAN AND OTHER PACIFIC ISLANDER
18.30%	(18.3)	HISPANIC OR LATINO (OF ANY RACE)
2.50%	(181)	TWO OR MORE RACES
8.50%	(614)	SOME OTHER RACE

ACKNOWLEDGEMENTS
The proposal for a New Jersey Greenway was initially developed in the context of several seminars at Princeton University taught by Mario Gandelsonas starting in 2008. The research took as a point of departure the 2006 project for the South Amboy Greenway by Agrest and Gandelsonas and was further expanded in 2009 as a project for a National Slow Infrastructure in a *charrette* that included Steve Lauritano and Chris Hillyard. The project conceived as a National plan for Greenways was designed to complement the "America 2050" megaregions proposed by the Regional Plan Association and based itself on Gandelsonas' text "Slow Infrastructure" which was presented at the conference "Metropoles en Miroir" sponsored by the Institut d'Edtudes Avances, Paris. The initial development of the New Jersey Greenway presented in this book, took place during the summer of 2010 in an intensive *charrette* based on the workshop "Fast/ Slow, Hard/Soft" organized by CAUI (the Center for Architecture, Urbanism and Infrastructure) earlier that year. The working group that included Philip Tidwell, Matthew Clarke, Phoebe Springstubb, and Sam Stewart-Halevy began to develop the New Jersey Greenway at the scale of the state as well as the proposals for the individual towns. In 2011 Philip Tidwell developed the set of drawings describing America 2050 including the National Slow Infrastructure and began the work of consolidating the many drawings and images into the design of this publication. Willem Boning completed work on the drawings for towns located in the northern section of the New Jersey Greenway while Stephanie Lee and Lydia Xynogala revised and completed drawings of the 12 New Jersey towns. Cong Wang provided essential statistical research and gathered background material for the completion of the project drawings.